I write books that help people start a part-time business working from their home. My part is to research products and companies and to provide *facts* so you might make an "informed decision" to see if this business is right for you—or not.

First, I look for a PRODUCT that people either want or need that they use over and over again. Next I look for corporate officers who have integrity, are experienced and who have money. Then, how much can *you* earn in this business? And last, how do you learn about this business and can YOU do it?

I have found a business that has EVERYTHING you need to be successful (and have FUN doing). I respect, believe in and LIKE those running this company. If you'll read what I've researched and ACT —you have a CHANCE to be successful.

The last chapter of this book talks about MONEY. That's what you're looking for, isn't it? I can't *guarantee* that you will be successful, but the only reason you won't is if you don't try.

Please read this entire book. It could change your financial life forever and help you . . .

SHOOT for the STARS

SHOOT

for the

ST★RS

TRAVEL, HAVE FUN, MAKE MONEY AND HELP OTHERS

YOURTRAVELBIZ.COM

Pete Billac

Swan Publishing

Author: Pete Billac
Editors: Steve Sturgeon, Dr. Rudolph Hebert
Cover Design: John Gilmore
Layout Design: Sharon Davis

OTHER BOOKS BY PETE BILLAC:

The Annihilator
How Not to Be Lonely—TONIGHT
The Last Medal of Honor
All About Cruises
New Father's Baby Guide
Willie the Wisp
Managing Stress
Justice is Green
Natural Air
Your Home-Based Business (And how to make it WORK)

Copyright @ January 2007 Swan Publishing
Library of Congress Catalog Card # 2006910533
ISBN# 0-943629-59-4
ISBN# 978-0-943629-59-9

SHOOT FOR THE STARS is available in quantity discounts through SWAN Publishing, 1059 CR 100, Burnet, TX 78611.

e-mail: swan@swan-pub.com
Phone: (512) 756-6800 Fax: (512) 756-0102

Printed in the United States of America.

FOREWORD

I've *struggled* with this FOREWORD trying to say the right words. I've changed it, erased it completely, put back some of the parts of it, changed it again, and decided to just DO IT and hope for the best!

I have NEVER, absolutely NEVER, found such a total "package" that gives you a chance to change your financial life forever. After you read this book you truly CAN make that "informed decision" I mention on the page as you opened this book.

I KNOW about these businesses; I've been "around them" for more than FOUR decades. I've watched companies succeed and I've watched them NOT succeed. I've been friends with many who HAVE made a success in this business, and I have listened to the moans and groans from those who failed.

Yes, more than forty years I've visited with, vacationed with and become friends with several hundred who made more money working from their home than they could spend in a lifetime.

I have some of those stories, and tell you how they did it. I also explain why so many FAIL in this business. I feel you can learn from the good as well as the bad—just follow the good.

Pete Billac

DISCLAIMER

I am not paid by any company or individual to write this book; I did it on my own. I researched it carefully, and if any figures or names are not correct, it is not intentional.

I encourage you to get more information from the person giving you this book and if any of my facts are incorrect, I would appreciate if you would contact me and I promise to change it in the rewrite.

Author

DEDICATION

To Coach, Scott and Kim, three visionaries who have made business—FUN. You'll meet each of them in this book; they are exceptional human beings.

Scott, Coach and Kim

INTRODUCTION

Let's visit a bit so you'll know who I am, what I do, and WHY this book should be of interest to most of you. This is my 58th book; 46 have sold over one million copies each. Nobody knows me; I write about a variety of topics on whatever interests me, and then hope my books appeal to "the masses."

I have books on adventure, relationships, the Mafia, cruises, the justice system, a baby guide for new fathers, gambling on the Internet, a light-heavy-weight boxing champion, a Medal of Honor recipient, how to buy a new car, gardening, indoor polluted air, building and remodeling your home, health, weight loss, managing stress, and a rewrite on one titled YOUR HOME-BASED BUSINESS.

I have FUN writing books and I try to make even a *business book* read like a novel. My writing style is not correct; my goals are solely for SUBSTANCE and COMMUNICATION. And if I repeat myself a time or two, I promise it's not *Alzheimer's,* it's something that I feel NEEDS repeating.

This book has few, if any, BIG words in it. If I do come across one of these words (once I understand what they mean), I change them so "ordinary humans" can read it without having earned a PhD or with a dictionary at their side.

My books are in large print and I put emphasis on words using CAPITALS, **bold**, *italics,* "quotation marks"— dashes and (parentheses). Pure writers, avid readers, EDITORS, English teachers, critics and grammarians *(most of whom have never written a* *book)shriek* over this and send letters to me telling me what a terrible writer I am; that I have *dangling participles* and *gerund phrases*; I don't even know what those ARE!

When one of my books hits the millionth mark in sales and I pass a mirror, I look in, smile and just about *spit all over myself* I'm so happy. I must have done some good things in my life to be blessed with the ability to write *wrong* and have people buy my books. No bragging, you understand, FACT!

I like short books because *my* "attention span" is short and I have much to do. I'm fast, and I'm also candid. If I offend anyone, I apologize in advance. My chosen "mission" is to get facts and to relay them to those who are looking *for* facts.

I want to share with you the results of my research into this company and the people behind this company, and how YOU have a chance to make a lot of money.

Yes, I look for product first, but like a racehorse, you also need a jockey, trainers and a path to follow. I have discovered it all. Let's begin.

TABLE OF CONTENTS

*"If you think you CAN,
or think you CAN'T, you're RIGHT!"*

COMMON SENSE

WHY THE TRAVEL BUSINESS

If I seem to harp on "product," it's because to make a lot of money in *any* business, you sincerely need a GOOD product. Without a product that "the masses" want, need, or use, your chance of success *diminishes*. In the words of *Paul Harvey: "NOW for the REST of the story!"*

In 2003, a wealthy entrepreneur named *Barry Diller* bought *Expedia* (online travel agency) for 5.1 **BILLION** dollars. BEFORE this huge purchase by *Mr. Diller*, Coach, Scott and Kim (innovators and corporate heads of YTB) had started their *own* travel business. This huge purchase by *Mr. Diller* made them feel more certain that they were on the right track.

So, these YTB people knew that their "product" was good, but where's the vehicle to "move" this product? They were already working on this. And their story is a truly splendid one.

I'll introduce the ones behind this business as we move along in this book. For now, let's look more into what YTB is doing with *their* "vehicle."

ADVERTISING

After forking over 5.1 BILLION dollars for this Online travel company, Mr. Diller had to find a way to get people TO the web site. This isn't easy.

For instance, I was researching a book on plastic surgery. There are over a MILLION web sites to chose from. HOW will Mr. Diller get people to look at HIS site? His answer: ADVERTISING!

Advertising is one of the "necessary evils" in any business. How DO you get people into your "web?" Mr. Diller is spending five MILLION dollars a WEEK to advertise! THAT'S how you draw people to your particular site; you "hammer" them with costly ads.

With YTB you have the SAME advantages, the SAME competitive prices, the same EVERYTHING as this rich entrepreneur, and it costs them NOTHING to advertise.

HOW CAN THIS BE? Mr. Diller certainly must know what these three YTB corporate heads know. Apparently not, or he has taken a different path. This "path" with YTB is one that YOU can take to go into business for yourself and SUCCEED.

NEVER SELL

There are many people who do not like network marketing (or multi-level marketing) because they are asked to SELL their friends, neighbors, relatives and everybody they meet.

And chances are great that you have friends (neighbors and relatives) who have tried to sell you "stuff" that you just weren't interested in buying.

And, these "sellers of stuff" pushed, tried to obligate, intimidate, and actually pestered you trying to SELL you, and you ran from them as if they had Yellow Fever. NOT THIS TIME! I would never suggest that you do that and have people hide from you.

Travel is a product that almost everyone uses. Grownups often look forward to travel and vacations as kids do on their first trip to the circus. And you just TELL—NEVER sell. You keep your friends and everybody's happy.

YTB's advertising is done by "word of mouth." It's the exact same as when you tell a friend about a good restaurant, hair stylist, great movie or competent doctor. They will listen if you aren't trying to SELL anything.

"People LOVE to BUY, but absolutely HATE being sold."

A DEAL

My mother-in-law had $300,000 in her personal checking account, but she drove 250 miles from the ranch in West Texas (and back) to a department store in Houston to SAVE twenty-five bucks on a refrigerator that was on sale. The GAS cost more than she saved.

Talking about GAS, I have a friend who is well-off, but he will drive across San Antonio to buy gas that is three CENTS per gallon cheaper. He figures he got a DEAL! It cost him MORE to get there than the money he saved.

Everyone, no matter how wealthy, likes a deal. How would YOU like to take flights to vacation spots around the world at competitive prices? And when you TELL others about the same "deal" you earn a commission at the same time.

How would you like to start your own home-based business with a PRODUCT that is outstanding? Travel IS that product. And, close to MAKING money is SAVING money. I think most of the people in the world like a deal; I know that I do.

I took my family on a cruise last year that cost about $9,000. Had I known about YOUR TRAVEL BIZ then, I could have saved as much as TWENTY FIVE PERCENT! (Hindsight is always 20/20).

Yet another high point about YTB is that it is extremely EASY; you just TELL others about your travel deal, lead them to your web site, they punch a few keys and book their flight, cruise, hotel, etc. It's all there before them. They can even "walk through" the hotel and see exactly what it looks like before they book it. And YOU do nothing! Just wait for your check.

What can be easier than punching a few keys on your computer and booking it ALL? And, what a terrific way to earn money; helping others while you help yourself. THAT'S A DEAL!

THE BIG DEAL

It's unthinkable that YTB was able to get the SAME "deal" as Barry Diller offers on the Internet. But it's TRUE! It took some smart thinking, maneuvering, action, perseverance and substantial money but NOT 5.1 billion dollars.

The YTB "booking engine" is similar to Mr. Diller's but YTB paid $30,000 down and $700 per month for a franchise booking engine from REZconnect. They then upgraded it with **"a few million bucks"** and can deliver it to YOU over your computer with the push of a few keys.

Yes, YTB has the SAME destinations and discounts on flights, cruises, and hotels. And YOU, as a YTB Referring Travel Agent (RTA), can begin earning a commission on anyone you "lead" to YOUR web site.

Most families spend about $4,000 on vacations each year. If just 10 families book their vacations on your website each year, you will earn between $1,500 and $4,000.

Plus, **I'LL** help you with your business, if you're willing to put forth effort, and *ask* for my help. I am always available, and my help is FREE. Just e-mail me for FREE information. Are you INTERESTED in finding out more?

WHY THIS BUSINESS

It just MAKES SENSE! You have a "product" that most of the world uses, you get competitive prices, and it is so outrageously easy. What REALLY excites me is that all you have to do is TELL others (friends, neighbors, relatives, anyone and everyone you meet) about how you can get them flights, cruises, hotels, rental cars, and then direct them to your web site. The COMPUTER does the rest.

The computer takes down all the records and YOU get a check each week. Not only do YOU do very little, but THEY do very little, and it's easy for them to do by just hitting a few keys.

YTB is "the" most outstanding company that I have seen, EVER. It's a win-win-win situation. YTB makes money, YOU make money (save money on travel), and you help OTHERS.

And, since TRAVEL is so interesting and exciting to TELL about, EVERYONE listens and you just TELL. I can't believe it's so very EASY. If you don't "make it" in this business, you either didn't learn how to do it, or you didn't TRY.

Do you understand what I'm telling you? You have the PRODUCT that people spend SEVEN TRILLION dollars a year using, they use it over and over again, you TELL and never SELL, and the COMPUTER does the bookkeeping for you.

You need NO prior training; YTB will teach you what to do and HOW to do it. All YOU Have to do is be able to READ and LISTEN. You can start it in your spare time, do most of it from your home, and it costs very little to start.

As I see it, you have two options; try it or stay with your JOB. I want this book to GIVE you the option of having a chance to become financially successful.

ANY BUSINESS COSTS MONEY

Even if you're in the lawn-care business you'll need tools (mower, weed eater, edger, shovels, a TRUCK, etc.) and HOW do you find customers? THEN you have to WORK, and that work is not easy and no fun.

If you start something big, like a McDonald's or Wendy's, we're talking about hundreds of thousands of dollars for the franchise alone, maybe more than a MILLION dollars.

And there's a dozen other expenses; insurance, equipment, help, inventory and the building itself. If you are able to BORROW the money, add the interest on that. Whew! You have to sell more than a few MILLION hamburgers to even get your initial investment back.

You can't even get a Krispy Kream (donut) franchise unless you have a five MILLION dollar financial statement. I know if I had that much money, I would NOT try to make more by selling DONUTS!

Let's go "smaller, because you don't have a lot of money to invest. How much does it cost to get into this business? I'm not telling you. I don't want you to even think about the cost at this juncture.

What I WILL tell you is that it costs very little and that ANYONE can afford it. I'll let the person who gave you this book give you that information. You will be pleasantly surprised, I promise. Let me tell you about some things in life we all have to make . . .

CHOICES

I don't mean to philosophize, but the only choices in life that you cannot make is in choosing your parents. Everything else you choose. If you choose correctly, good things usually happen. If you choose INcorrectly bad things can happen.

There are three "tracks" to take if you are interested in starting a business from your home. Track ONE is you can look for another business other than this one.

Track TWO is when you can become an RTA (Referring Travel Agent) with YTB. You can start a career from your home that puts you IN one of the travel businesses. Or Track THREE, stay with your JOB.

I called Ron Head who has been with YTB as a REP and as an RTA for about four years. I telephoned Ron because I was at a meeting where he was presented a *REP bonus check* for one MILLION dollars! I SAW THE CHECK!

"Pete, this company is magnificent," Ron told me. *"The owners are close friends of mine, they have*

'paid the price' these past five years of sticking with their business. Coach sold his 'dream house' to help fund this company.

"There is no easier less expensive, FUN business in the world to start a home-based business working PART TIME than these travel businesses. If they get involved with YTB they are on the right track."

The three "tracks" I mention are fact. It's up to you to make that choice. If I knew of a better choice, I'd tell you about it. So it's up to you as to which track to take. Will Rogers said . . .

"Being on the right track is fine,
but if you just sit and wait,
a train comesalong and runs you over."

OTHER PRODUCTS

There are thousands of new (MLM) companies starting each year; the greater majority of them CLOSE in that same year. Actually, MOST new companies "fold" within a year, you just don't hear about them. The main reason that most of these MLM companies never make it is because they don't have a good product.

They all LOOK for a product that is unique, that is a "consumable," that helps people in some way. Without that "product" your chance of making a living, part-time (or full-time) in a home-based business, lessens.

I've written a few books about companies with

"physical" products. I felt that their products were good ones and that they did what the company said they would do. And I have many successful friends who are involved with these companies. Here is one problem I have with this particular type of company.

Let's take the companies that market health food, vitamins, supplements, some type of pills or elixirs. Are these products "good?" I have no idea, and what's more, MOST of the people marketing this product have NO IDEA EITHER.

They are neither scientists nor nutritionist; they listen to what they are told, either by the person in front of the room or by the friend who enrolled them. And the "friend" only knew what THEY were told. So here's a bunch of people trying to SELL something they know NOTHING about. THAT is why I do my research.

Woefully, these folks truly BELIEVE what they are told and they will have testimonials from people who will SAY things like: *"It will cure cancer, diabetes, Alzheimer's, heart trouble, and grows HORNS ON CHICKENS!"*

When the FTC (Federal Trade Commission) "gets wind" of these false claims, and when they get several, they file suit and close the COMPANY. Who's to blame? The distributors who MAKE these false claims, or the company who tries to market a product that doesn't work? Who cares? Your big concern is that you are OUT OF BUSINESS!

Of the top 30 home-based business companies

in the world, 20 of them are health related. This is impressive. It stands to reason that with so many successful companies selling these products that it must be a good business for you.

The problem is, the COMPETITION is so strong that the purchaser doesn't know WHAT to believe or what to buy. There are people "coming at them" from all directions telling why their product is better than the rest. What CAN they believe?

Plus, some of the companies that are "struggling" have ONE "lead product" and sell other products that you can buy at Wal*Mart at about one fifth the cost!

I did research on TABLETS. Do you know that the number ONE "ingredient" (other than the obvious) found in hospital bedpans, port-o-potties, and septic tanks are vitamin TABLETS!

LOOK at the coating; they use the same for "fillers" in these tablets as they use to make BUTTONS! You need a hammer to break these things and your body can't dissolve them unless you have a GIZZARD!

And, these supplement companies compel you (or you make NO commission) to buy their products each month. Usually, you can't consume all of these "things" yourself, and if you don't SELL them you store them in your closet or garage.

The main ones who benefit from this "stuff" (if it does in fact work) are rats and roaches. And, as I say jokingly, the only way to get your money back is to insure the garage and BURN IT DOWN!

I don't mean to "knock" or dissuade you from selling vitamins, tonics or supplements because some of these really ARE good; YOU just have to find out which ones. Get the wrong supplements, the wrong information, and if they don't sell or you can't consume them yourself, call your insurance man.

GUINEA PIG TEAM

I've written books on health products. I've looked at, researched and investigated hundreds of companies and their products. This is how I determined that these products were valid. You'll laugh, but it's FACT!

First, I try the product to see if I get any results. If I feel a *difference*, I then go to my "Guinea Pig Team" comprised of seven friends who will try ANYTHING as long as it's FREE!

If THEIR results are positive, I then send the "health stuff" to dieticians, nutritionists, health experts and physicians who study nutrition and who know about and understand the benefits of actual vitamin supplements. I PAY these people to report FACTUAL information.

Of the hundreds I've "looked at," the dozens I've investigated in depth, I've written a book on but TWO! I like neither the competition nor the odds. That's why I look for a product that is first or unique. This "travel business" might not be first, but it certainly IS unique, and YOU are on the right track.

THIS BUSINESS

The YTB companies offer two unique and powerful business opportunities, that of referring travel agent or 'RTA' and that of independent marketing representative or 'REP.' There is no fee or RTA purchase required to be a REP. One may choose to participate in one or both opportunities.

TRENDS are important to look for to build a successful business. To get "ahead" of these trends is smart. With this business, travel and with YTB you ARE ahead of the trend. YTB saw this trend (apparently) a few years BEFORE Mr. Diller saw it.

When business people tell you that *"You are in the right place at the right time."* they don't especially mean with the COMPANY; they are specifically talking about the TREND.

Also, MOST companies have a "growing period" in that it takes TIME to get everything in place. It isn't necessary to be FIRST in a new company. In fact, if the company was at the beginning of a trend, that's terrific. But their "growth" doesn't truly start for a few years.

YTB had a *"growth period"* that took a few years of "trying," and after spending a lot of money for answers, they have "arrived!" YOU are now, *"at the right place at the right time."* Let's LOOK AT their amazing growth.

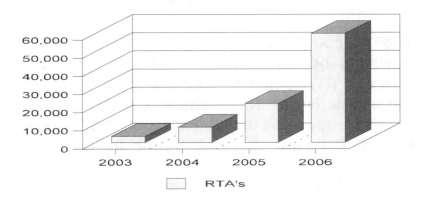

RTA's

From all that seems plausible, their 60,000 associates should double again in 2007, maybe more. THIS means that you ARE "at the right place at the right time." And if the travel prognosticators are right, the worldwide travel business will be at or around FOURTEEN trillion dollars in the next several years.

In the month of September 2006, a YTB REP with more than six total group RTA sales earned an average of over $1,400 in one month.

THESE BUSINESSES make sense because of all the "figures" I have marked down. Plus, by working with a computer, there IS no "stuff" to store, no "back orders," lost orders, incorrect amounts or damaged goods. There is no STACKING boxes, carrying them to meetings, trade shows etc. It's all done with a few keys being pushed.

I'm hoping this makes sense to you. I'm just telling you the way it is. Yes, I've written books on companies who market "physical" products and there are many successful people doing this. But why not find a product that is easier and FUN to TELL about, a product that is into the TRILLIONS?

HOW YOU CAN DO THIS

Many people NEED more money, and most people just do not HAVE millions, hundreds of thousands and maybe not even enough to start that lawn-care business I talked about earlier.

If you go to a bank to borrow money, you must HAVE money in order to BORROW money. With THIS business you don't NEED a college diploma, not even a high school education, or ANY prior training. And you don't NEED a lot of money.

You don't NEED an office or helpers. You don't NEED to drive your car to work. This is your OWN business that you work from HOME. In fact, you can work in your pajamas or sweats, naked even, unless you have neighbors and relatives who just "drop by."

All you DO need is a telephone, a computer, access to the Internet, and put forth effort by TELLING others about it. Then you'll need a little money for postage, telephone bills, and the Internet access fee. *Peanuts*! But, you know this; it takes SOME money to make money.

If you don't have a computer, GET ONE! They're cheap. If you don't understand how to use a computer, it's easy. I'M a computer "dunce." I can send e-mails, find out the weather when I travel overseas (or from Texas to Minnesota), titles and times for movies and look up info on *Google*.

That's IT! With your computer, you can send a message or letter to thousands in minutes. I learned to do these things in ONE HOUR! Since my brain works from a different side than most of you who have even a degree of technical know-how, you can learn how to do it in a HALF hour!

PLUS, the "tax advantages" of owning your own home-based business MORE than makes up for what you have to spend. If you don't know what they are, ask the person who gave or sent you this book; THEY will know!

All you truly HAVE TO DO is to "find" at least 10 hours a week, LEARN about the business, and TELL others how to find your web site. If you spend fewer hours, you might earn a few dollars. If you spend more hours, you have a chance to make more.

I have NEVER seen a company, product and a home-based business that has EVERYTHING! Don't panic, I'll tell you about it ALL in the chapters ahead. For now, please read why I'm doing this. Here is . . .

Chapter 2

MY STORY

Having lived a full life, my background often *runs parallel* with the lives of many, and I'm hoping that some of you can "identify" my life with yours. This will help us to sort of "bond."

Coach and I had so many "*threads*" (so MUCH in common and how closely our lives paralleled) that it was uncanny. Apparently I sort of like *myself*, so I *had* to like Coach. When I tell you about HIS life, you will be awestruck. Now, I'll tell you about mine.

My parent's were poor; my dad was a house painter and my mom a housewife. My dad worked EVERY DAY for 45 years, sick or not. The DAY he retired he *had* to find another job.

I didn't realize HOW poor we were until I went to school and found that my classmates ALL had toilets that were INSIDE. And most had clothes that were *not* bought from *Spiegel's* or *Sears* catalogs.

No tears, please. My parents loved me, taught me about God, about being kind, about telling the truth and to help others. But I vowed way back then when I was about 11 that I'd do whatever necessary to NOT be poor when I became a grownup.

DEAD BROKE

Any of you ever been in this situation? It's no fun, is it? No, it's no fun being poor, but it's DEVASTATING to be rich then *become* poor. This happened to ME!

As an adult I had some fun, reasonably wild years and made a substantial amount of money. I wrote for sitcoms, did a few movies, risked my life doing some absolutely dumb things but invested wisely and then—it all came to an end.

It was the early 1980's when I had my money "spread all over" so my chances of losing it ALL would be slim. HOWEVER, literally ALL of those I had invested in had failed businesses and went broke. When they couldn't pay me, I couldn't pay the ones I owed. I took bankruptcy!

Oh, some of my "run-around buddies" still had money and were willing to "pay my way" but, *"When you can't run with the pack, you have to leave the pack."* I owed almost a million dollars.

Those I owed money didn't want a "story;" they loaned me money for a beachfront home, cabin cruiser, gold Mercedes, and other "toys" some grown-ups have.

I was called several times a day, EVERY day, for months. *"Can you pay $50 a week or $25 a week?"* they would ask. I was nice to the callers no matter how aggravating; they were only doing their job. But I didn't HAVE $50 or $25. I had "rat-holed" some money but not much. Has this ever happened to you?

At bankruptcy court I was standing beside such notables as Texas Governor John Connolly and world renowned heart surgeon, Dr. Denton Cooley. I invested in many of the same "ventures" as they had, and we ALL went bust.

However, Dr. Cooley could operate on a few heart patients and make a million back. Governor Connolly had been in politics many years and some of his "oil rich" buddies bought *his* ranches back for him. The only "asset" I had was a half-completed manuscript on a book titled HOW NOT TO BE LONELY.

Everyone in court (including the judge) laughed at the title. The court filed a lien against everything, but left me with my Mercedes and what they deemed NOT an asset—the book.

After feeling sorry for myself for those first seven days, trying to blame everyone and everything under the sun for this "predicament" I was in, I looked in the mirror at the true culprit. I made up my mind to get out of this mess I had created and knew that . .

"If it is to be, it is up to ME!"

WHAT TO DO NOW

I had two strong motivating factors to get out of this *situation*; hunger and loss of dignity; in that order. So, I set up a plan to do it.

It took a month before my assets were taken. Looking out of the large glass doors of my condo at the beautiful lake, I sighed, smiled, reached for my positive attitude and set out to "make it" again. I decided to *"plan my work, and work my plan."*

Rent was high in Houston and I had "some" cash, so I was able to rent a very small house in a little country town in East Texas in the *Piney Woods*. My "plan" was to finish my . . . Lonely book.

I couldn't get a job that made sense; I owed almost a million dollars! What kind of job could I get to earn that much money? The book was my only answer. I went to work finishing the book.

LOVE CONQUERS ALL

My girlfriend and I had been together for almost three years. We had vacationed all over the world, ate at fine restaurants, attended plays, dinner parties, etc. We enjoyed somewhat of a "movie star" life during those "good" years. I was rich, remember?

We traveled to *Russia, Germany, Spain, Paris, Norway, England* and *Monte Carlo*. We vacationed on the *Gold Coast in Australia*, sailed on the *Adriatic*, and prayed at *St. Marks Cathedral* in *Venice*.

And, after I had ZERO, she *"stuck with me!"* Also, she had $10,000 in her savings account that she handed over to me; this had to "last" until I could finish my book. It would take a few months.

We learned to be "careful" with that money. It was nearing Christmas, and with "straining funds" I cut down a small cedar tree that she decorated with one string of lights she bought at Wal*Mart, and we got moss from trees as "fillers."

It has, to this day, been the most delightful, happy Christmas we had ever shared. And that Christmas *tree* will be remembered over all others. We had little money left, but we dropped $100 in the offering plate at church. We loved each other and truly, "*love conquers all.*"

DEAL OR NO DEAL

During the "good" years, neither of us worked. We would sit on the balcony of my condo in swimsuits watching the sailboat races while drinking lemonade and playing *Backgammon.* Evenings we'd relax and watch *Wheel of Fortune* and compete for answers; we are both competitive.

Even the antique *Backgammon* set "went" to creditors. Now, our *whole world* had changed. Now, all we had was a checker board we bought at a garage sale for fifty cents.

I worked on my book maybe 10 to 14 hours a day, EVERY day. She went to work (not a lot of jobs to be had there) at a flea market. Degrading? Of course, but better than starving, and she believed in me and that silly book.

Our "fun" together was walking in the woods, watching either of the THREE channels on TV (by turning the "rabbit ears" to different compass points), or playing checkers.

Of course, she'll deny my figures, but I must have won *three-hundred* games of checkers and she won about four or five at the most.

One day when she broke out the checker board, she wanted to make a bet with me she said . . .

"Let's do this. I love you and you love me. I (obviously) can't marry you for your money, and we've been together several years. I challenge you to a game of checkers. If YOU win I'll not bring it up again. But if I win, we marry soon, and you name the date.

That was fine with me; my odds of NOT losing were about 99 to 1. The game took less than THREE MINUTES and SHE won!

She had been "sandbagging" me for more than two YEARS. Well I named the date, April 1st, April Fool's Day four months away. She agreed.

Still with little or no money, we were married by a Justice of the Peace in a gazebo in the park. I had a few people present (can't even remember who) and had enough money to buy two gold wedding bands from a pawn shop.

NETWORK MARKETING

I had been researching my book for several years; I finished it in a few months. The problem now was, NOBODY would publish it and I was going to have to print it myself. HOW? I had NO MONEY.

My experience with network marketing helped. I made a *list* of everyone I knew, knew *of*, thought about, met, etc. BEFORE the book went to press. I called, e-mailed and wrote 1,700 people. It's amazing if you really think about it and make a list of just *how many* people we all know.

I had about 1,100 people who *pre-bought* the book at ten bucks each. That was enough money to print 3,000 books. The extra ones I had I sold, ordered more, sold them and it went on.

I even "network marketed" it in a fashion. I couldn't "duplicate" my own efforts, but kind of. I went to dozens of small stores within about a 10-mile radius of where I lived and left the books on consignment. The stores kept some money and I got some money.

I found a "ladies group" who liked me and THEY had several hundred CHAPTERS throughout the U.S. I gave THEM books on consignment; the book sold for $10 ($9.95) and they kept four. I had a "downline" without realizing it.

At the same time, my *wife* spent 8 to10 hours a day making telephone calls for more than two years setting up meetings for me to make speeches and sell the book.

I gave *677 speeches* that first year to anyone who would listen; *Lions, Kiwanis, Rotary, AARP, Mended Hearts, Bird Watchers, Flower groups, the 82nd Airborne, realtor's, breakfast groups, church groups*—ANYONE—and I sold books.

I went on hundreds of radio shows, made TV appearances on national shows and found out that people LISTENED to me. I mixed "stories" and jokes with my speeches; it WORKED! I was exhausted, but I LIKED what I was doing and I KNEW what I was talking about.

To make a long story short, I made three million dollars in the next few years, paid ALL my debts, and life was "good again."

WORK SMART

I always say that *smart* work, works better than *hard* work. Hard SMART work can't fail—IF you have a product that "the masses" want or need, and I was one "book-selling *sonofagun*." I LIKED it, and had but ONE product. THINK if I had a product (like YTB) that the "masses" use.

To me, it wasn't work at all; I played it like a game. In talking to groups I sort of "challenged myself" to get the "stone face" in the crowd to laugh—maybe even just smile. I "played my game" trying to raise my percentage of sales. I got better at speaking, and within three months I sold about 85% of those in attendance. YOU do the same. LEARN this business and TELL everyone about it.

I remember coming home with the money and throwing it in the center of the bed. It started with a hundred or so per day, then a thousand. Then I was able to charge for appearances AND sell books. My fees went from $50, to $100 to $500 and to five THOUSAND. And in a few years even MORE.

ONE WORD DID IT

WOMEN bought that HOW NOT TO BE LONELY book about 1,000 to 1 over men. The sub-title said, *"HOW to find mate, WHERE to look, WHAT to say, and HOW to keep them."* Men just don't read that kind of stuff.

I decided to market to the MEN, and changed the title with but ONE word—TONIGHT. The same book, HOW NOT TO BE LONELY TONIGHT sold seven MILLION copies, enough for me to retire forever! REMEMBER . . .

"It's not how many times you get knocked down, It's how many times you get back UP!"

It IS all up to you; if you *desire* to make more money, you make an *"academic choice"* on a business and then to DO it. I don't mean to dwell on *me* and *my stories*, I'm just hoping that many of you have *"been there"* too, and that you can *identify* with these stories.

YOUR BUSINESS

If I have to say it time and again, the PRODUCT is so important. And the COMPANY is very close behind. If you truly WANT to be financially successful, few ever accomplish that working for someone else.

THAT'S why this business with YTB caught my

attention. I heard about it; it made sense. I took the time to visit with the corporate heads and I LIKED THEM more than you can imagine.

I looked at their REP and RTA pay plans, their training and how truly "real" these folks were. I saw the faces in the crowd at a meeting they held on Red Carpet Days. I'll tell you more about that as we move ahead with the story.

I saw how those in the audience acted and reacted. When Coach's son, Scott, spoke—these folks listened intently; I listened. But more than that, I WATCHED the faces of the others. It was like one large FAMILY. So many of these MLM companies call themselves a "family" and/or try to get this type of family, but they never seem to be able to do it.

I spoke with many in that audience and listened to their stories of beginning hardships and how they were able to really "make it" in this business.

I learned that the Level 2 Directors EACH get a bonus of $50,000. I saw Ron and Judy Head get their one MILLION DOLLARS! Yes, I SAW THE CHECK!

And Rick and Brenda Ricketts and P.J. (Pete) Jensen are due THEIR million buck *bonus* around Christmas time of THIS year! A MILLION DOLLAR **BONUS** CHECK. What other company does THAT?

And I saw some new REPs who sat with eyes bulging, hoping they could do the same. I feel that ALL could do it if they TRY. Some are in a financial RUT. This is what I know.

*"The difference between a rut and a grave,
is that a rut has TWO WAYS OUT."*

THIS business truly is a way OUT of any financial situation you might be in. You have to WANT to change your financial life, you have to LEARN how to do it (they'll teach you), and then you have to DO IT! The truth is . . .

ANYBODY CAN DO IT

I feel that most people want to be *appreciated.* I absolutely grin from ear to ear and it "warms my heart" when people call and *thank me* for helping them. But more than *that*, I'm hoping that my research, and the stories about me and those behind this company, will "reach" you and help you get out of whatever *rut* you might be in.

I want to try and convince you that failing is nothing new; that being in a rut is commonplace. If you want to change things, YOU are the only one who can DO SOMETHING about it. YTB is that chance, and if you learn and TRY, failing is not an option.

Part of my reason for wanting to write this book, about THIS company is because I can find NO FLAWS in their planning and their direction. They ARE "good people" and this is important to me, and also to YOUR success.

BROKEN HEARTS

I sincerely DO care about others. I KNOW the broken hearts, busted marriages, anguish and pain caused when a company closes and their employees suffer. I remember ENRON, and I *hurt* for these people.

I've seen so very many who *believed* (I was living in Houston when the end came) and I KNEW a few dozen of the people who lost their entire LIFE SAVINGS. I'm tough, in that if a cannonball hit me in the head it would bounce off.

But my heart was literally *shattered* when so many hard-working, honest, *good* people who spent their lives with ENRON ended up BROKE. All those years they worked for this company and invested in it, and it was gone in an instant.

THAT is another reason that I research like *Columbo.* I get the facts and tell them to you straight so you can make that "informed decision" and build a future for yourself. I do NOT want you to make a mistake with the wrong product and/or the wrong company.

Remember, I'm not being PAID by anyone to write this book, and I am not trying to *sell* you anything other than to SELL you on YTB. These businesses have EVERYTHING for you to become financially successful.

But, please, don't let me "talk" you into anything. Read this book. Pay CLOSE ATTENTION to my last chapter on MONEY. Read the YTB *Success* magazine, listen to tapes, watch the videos, ASK questions, then ACT! I remember the saying:

"Give a person a fish and feed them for a day. TEACH them to fish and feed him for a lifetime."

WHY I FEEL QUALIFIED

In this book, I am trying to teach you to fish. Being the best player doesn't qualify you to be a good coach. I "played" in the network marketing business years ago and didn't like it; it was *different* then. But it changed (thank goodness).

I didn't want to sell soap or vitamins. I didn't like having to pursue (coerce, SELL, trick, obligate, pester, intimidate) others to BUY my products. I wanted to be their friend and not have them hide when they saw me.

Many who COULD do this and stayed with it made really BIG money. Many of those started their own MLM companies and many failed. Others "hung around" waiting until the business changed. I've "watched" all of this happen.

I've known, known of, visited with and become friends with hundreds who were (and are) in their own home-based business. I know their stories; I've watched them and I learned *from* them. I bring ALL that knowledge to you.

I have "been around" network marketing for more than forty years. I have seen dozens of companies make it, and *thousands* fail. I knew several hundred distributors/members/associates who earned more money than they dreamed existed, thousands who were "*comfortable*," and many *more* who made ZERO.

I knew ALL the mistakes these companies that failed had made, other than a faulty product. I saw them write incorrect information, CHANGE their marketing plan (either stupid, greedy or BOTH), and crooks in corporate "run with the money." THAT'S why the research that I do is so valuable to you.

Remember, too, I don't just write a book and sail away on my yacht to *Tahiti*, I "work" the book and spend a lot of time HELPING YOU with this business.

I'm doing what I LIKE, and (unashamedly spoken) I'm GOOD at it! I don't mean to boast and "*blow my own horn*." But, "*I'M the only one driving this car*." I felt that I NEEDED to tell you WHY I feel qualified to give you advice, and I'm doing it because I LIKE DOING IT!

I want to help YOU, and I'm hoping that the majority of you can "identify" with some of my background, problems and successes. It's these people (Coach, Scott, Kim, Ron, Rick, P.J., Juliet) and a few others that I want to spotlight.

THEY are the ones I want you to know. THEY are the ones who will help you—directly change your life and lifestyle for the better.

Chapter 3

YOUR LIFE and FUTURE

There truly is so much to say that I'm STILL not certain where to put what. For now, let's talk about what you *have* and what you *could have*. My last chapter (about money) might be the BEST part of this book. But let's talk here about . . .

A J.O.B.

I don't mean to "fault" those of you for having a job; most of the people in the world have a job and they are necessary for this world to survive. I just feel that what is termed "normal" is lacking.

We are taught to get an education, get a JOB, marry, have kids, bring them to adulthood, hopefully become a grandparent—then die!

That's the "normal" *life cycle* most people go through. But now there are OPTIONS and you can start on a part-time basis trying to be your own boss.

I'm teaching my two sons (Clay is 11, and Brad is 13) about business. I train them to eat healthy, to love God, to be polite and to make money; not necessarily in that order. I want them to work for themselves.

I don't want a BOSS yelling at them, or them having to work for a *nincompoop*, or to be downsized or cut loose because the BOSS makes multiple mistakes. I want THEM to be "*the masters of their own fate.*"

I'm not trying to depress any of you who HAVE a job, but chances are the DAY you retire, your standard of living drops and/or you have to go back to work. That's what happened to MY father.

My dad painted houses for a living for 45 years. The very DAY he retired he had to look for another JOB. He worked at a JOB that paid LINEAR INCOME; when HE stopped pushing that paintbrush, the money stopped coming in. That's the way it is with most JOBS.

I'm trying to help those of you who want to be your OWN boss, to become financially independent, to find a business that gives you the best CHANCE possible to reach that goal. This book will tell you HOW to do that.

I don't want you to get up early, DRIVE to your JOB in heavy traffic, and if you get sick or tired or just don't FEEL like working to HAVE to work. I want "mom" there when the kids get off from school; no relative or babysitter or nanny can do what mom does. And I want dad to spend time WITH his wife and kids; that's a HOME and not a house.

With a job, you truly DO help "the boss" make money (or more money). And there is hardly ever any security; your JOB could end tomorrow for any number of reasons. There is no security by working for someone else; MY security is ME!

Many companies are downsizing, laying people off, forcing retirement (at a lesser payout on pensions). There are statistics that point out that past the age of 65 about 95 percent need RFC; HELP from relatives, friends and charity.

Yes, FEW get rich while working for someone else. MY part is to give you options, and I sincerely do want to help you if you are willing to TRY.

I want you to have a home-based business, at least on a part-time basis. When you earn THREE times your regular salary for SIX months in a row, if you want you can QUIT your J.O.B. (**J**ust **O**ver **B**roke) and go into your OWN business full time.

You see, your JOB pays what is termed LINEAR income; when YOU stop work, the MONEY stops. Let's look into the type of income I favor, and I'll tell you why. Let's find out the meaning of . . .

RESIDUAL INCOME

I've mentioned product several times, and will probably get "back" to it again. The product must be what "the masses" want or need. It must be relatively inexpensive to market, and it must be a consumable (or something that "the masses" use over and over again). THAT is what brings in RESIDUAL income.

Let me "touch" on HOW a good product works as far as RESIDUAL INCOME. I write books. MANY people read books. My books are listed on just about every computer in the world and are in thousands of book stores; some are in a dozen or more languages.

A few years back I went to the hospital for three days for a complete check-up. While I was AT the hospital, my books were selling. When I got out of the hospital, I had earned seventeen thousand dollars!

BECAUSE, I had a PRODUCT that "the masses" buy and I was earning RESIDUAL INCOME; the income that goes on and on if I'm asleep, on vacation, just don't "feel" like working or in the hospital for a check-up.

This doesn't happen EVERY three days, mind you, or I'd go back in the hospital for a YEAR! But it happens when you have a PRODUCT that is good. It can happen to you with these TRAVEL products.

This "word of mouth" stuff truly works. By TELL-ING others about your travel business, they save money and they in turn will tell others. It actually can go on and on and ON, and YOU make a REP or RTA commission EACH TIME anyone you tell, those they tell, and those THEY tell. This is called . . .

EXPONENTIAL GROWTH

In this business (YTB calls it REFERRAL MARKET-ING) you will hear the words "duplication" and "expo-nential." Let me tell you how POWERFUL these two words are. Here's my favorite "for instance" concerning exponential growth. It has to do with playing golf.

If you wager ONE PENNY on the first hole, then DOUBLE IT on the following 17 holes, that last BET is worth over TWELVE HUNDRED DOLLARS! Grab a calculator and see for yourself.

What this REALLY means is that if you TELL a few people each day and they tell a few who tell a few, SOON you'll have a lot of people who are working for themselves (but ALSO working for you) to help you succeed. It's so simple yet totally awesome.

By "telling" others and "training them" to tell others, you are duplicating your own efforts, and this exponential growth just happens. And your business can skyrocket.

HOW TO TURN FUN INTO FORTUNE

I don't like the word "work" because I don't feel that work is any FUN. I like a business that is FUN and also profitable, and that ANYONE CAN DO without a lot of money invested. I feel that I've FOUND it.

I apologize for "jumping around" in this book. I'm trying to tell you EVERYTHING but honestly, I am so EXCITED to have "found" YTB and the more I learn about it, the more passionate I get. I'm going to tell you more, and then there's even MORE that you can find out for yourself.

YTB teaches you how to become successful in these businesses and actually have FUN while doing them. THAT was my *mantra* before I met them. And the fact that this is what they teach brought me closer to them. There's "effort" involved. I often say that . . .

"If it was EASY to get rich, everybody would be rich."

    You WILL have to look and listen to audio tapes, videos, training sessions, conference calls, read their "Travel Book Toolbox," attend directors meetings, but there is no time limit. Nobody will "grade" you. If it takes you two weeks, or three, or MORE as long as you LEARN what to do, that's OK. Then all it takes is for you to DO IT!

    Coach is committed to this business. He was scheduled to catch the first ball for the 4th game of this years World Series with LOU BROCK throwing the pitch. Of course he's a *Cardinals* fan (they WON the series).

    He bypassed this honor to conduct a meeting for one of his REPs. These people CARE about their REPs and RTAs and you can get all the help you need just by ASKING FOR IT!

    But, it's up to you to ACT, STUDY and LEARN what you're talking about. How long will it take? It took me about a week. I'm not "knocking" a college education, but THAT takes FOUR years and when you graduate the first thing you do is LOOK for a J.O.B!

    With YTB you are in business for YOURSELF. In time you will build a following of customers, but your chance to bring in money immediately is there. This is a great spot to tell you about . . .

DUPLICATION

You can't "do it all" by yourself. YTB calls it *"Referral Marketing"* because that's how you become rich; by getting others to work *for* you. But they make money at the same time and they can do as you do and make MORE!

The best part of it all is that you "hire" these people and it costs you NOTHING. You "find" a few good people, you TRAIN them to do as you are doing, they train others and soon you could have hundreds, thousands, TENS of thousands working for you.

Here's another "for instance" on how DUPLICATION works. I helped a friend by doing a 30-minute radio show for him. To shorten this, he found but SEVEN people who stayed with his particular business.

With DUPLICATION (coupled with exponential growth) he had more than a MILLION people in his downline in ONE YEAR. Duplication happens when you train OTHERS to do as you have done, and when you help them, you also help YOURSELF.

If a person asked you whether you wanted ONE MILLION DOLLARS now, or the value of a penny that doubled itself in 30 days, MOST would "jump at" the million. The 30-day "doubling" yields **$10,737,418.24**. THAT is the power of EXPONENTIAL GROWTH!

THE BEGINNING STORY

It was around mid-August of 2006 when I received a telephone call from a man named *Steve Sturgeon*, a stranger to me. He had gotten my name from *Jenny Cassady*, a woman I met months ago when I was researching *another* company.

As I had done hundreds of times before, I listened. *"This company is special, Pete, unlike any other business in history,"* Steve told me, *"and you need to meet the man behind it all. He goes by the name of Coach. He is smart, honest, and has credibility and integrity; something rarely found in this business. He's really a good man."*

I had heard this many times before; EVERYONE feels that *their* business is *the* best one in mankind and the person in charge is special, and that everyone who gets involved can make millions. And they want me to write a book about it.

Steve gave me a web site that he wanted me to look over, and promised to mail me some more information. And, as I had done many times before, I went to the web site and looked to see what these "travel" businesses were all about.

I punched in *yourTravelBiz.com* and read some things that made sense. Within a few days I received a *SUCCESS* magazine in the mail from Steve with a CD enclosed. The magazine was *spectacular*, full of color photos and stories about the corporate officers, some background on them, and leaders in the company along with some useful information from several notables.

I read the entire magazine and smiled to myself; I felt that THIS might be a new book. I then shoved the CD in the slot on my computer and watched.

I learned that this company had *Priceline* and *Travelocity* where their associates could BOOK travel and EARN a commission with the push of a computer key. Next I had to learn WHAT this company, run by J. Lloyd *"Coach"* Tomer, (pronounced Tome-er), was doing and HOW they were doing it.

You recall my feelings; that PRODUCT is the main ingredient to look for in any home-based business. With that seven TRILLION dollars a year spent annually on travel, the product was there. SEVEN TRILLION! *Whew!* That's a lot of money.

When Steve called again, I told him that *the product* was spectacular, and that *now* I needed info on the corporate officers. Also, that I'd like to SEE the company to make certain it wasn't a *room* in an office with a *temp* answering the telephone.

Steve told me the only way to do this was to fly to St. Louis and meet Coach, see the corporate headquarters for myself and meet the people. He gave me two dates a few weeks ahead to choose from and said that HE would pay for my ticket.

I liked Steve the minute we shook hands at the airport in St. Louis. He was friendly and had a "way" about him, and he talked straight. I felt a bit guilty having Steve pay for my ticket, but I'll make it up to him in the future.

MY FIFTEEN MINUTES

I flew into St. Louis at about noon on a Wednesday. Steve and I checked into a motel and went directly to the offices that were large but rather crowded with people separated into small cubicles.

Sandy Pippins, Coach's "right hand" who is also Executive Vice President, told us that Coach stayed busy and that we have *fifteen minutes* with him.

I smiled at that, went to the rest room, looked in the mirror (again) to see if a *jackass* was looking back, and talked to myself.

"Do you mean that I have to drive a hundred miles from my ranch in Texas to the airport, go through all that trouble boarding a plane, repeat that on the way back and for FIFTEEN MINUTES?"

Well, I was HERE, so why not? I liked the travel business, their web site was exciting, and I heard so much about Coach from Steve that all I had to do was see the office, spend some time with Coach asking a few questions and decide to write this book. *The 15 minutes was acceptable.*

Coach *was* busy. He had 129 employees who were going to get "early" Christmas bonus checks at RED CARPET DAYS that "happens" every Thursday. They were expecting 200 to 300 or so people, they were treated to lunch at his country club and then would attend a meeting.

We waited about five minutes before being ushered upstairs to a meeting room with a large table and 10 or 12 chairs. I met Scott (Coach's son) and chatted with him for less than a minute. He exited knowing that I was there to interview Coach.

THE MEETING

Coach greeted me in his conference room with a wide smile and a firm handshake. I was dressed in slacks and long-sleeved shirt; Coach was wearing a polo shirt with a *St. Louis Cardinals* baseball jacket over it; on his feet were running shoes. He was comfortable and at ease. Steve was dressed like a bum.

"*But, NOBODY cares,*" Steve told me. "*The entire group are casual; they dislike suits with the exception of a few of the office folks.*" And Steve was just comfortable; you'll LIKE Steve.

Those fifteen minutes turned out to be over THREE HOURS—maybe FOUR! Coach and I liked each other instantly, and traded "war stories." It's really nice, isn't it, when you meet someone you like *immediately* and have many things in common? I think we'll become close friends. NO! I know it!

I feel I can "read" people well. He was friendly,  articulate (in a country-boy sort of way) and I could sense integrity In his face. He was excited about his business and he sacrificed much to get it to where it is now. This, I feel, is only the beginning of what will be a massive travel business soon to be the largest in the world.

J. Lloyd Tomer, founder and Chairman of the Board

I learned that Coach cared about people; REALLY cared. Again, so very many corporate officers SAY they care but rarely mean it; Coach DOES mean it! I knew that my first impression was "on target" about this really nice guy.

THE RIVER HOUSE

Our morning together started early. We met at the office about 8 am. Coach wanted me to see his house on the river. He, Steve and I, drove several miles to the banks of the Mississippi River and through an area with unbelievable mansions.

Of course, "a picture is worth a thousand

words." So here's "the house" we were visiting. It's called, *The River House*. I have to tell you about it. This black and white photograph does it no justice.

It was built in 1927 by the *Olin* family, the ones who own *Winchester* firearms. If you happen to own a gun and/or have any Winchester ammunition, look for the *Olin* name on the box.

The home is three stories high, a Southern Colonial home, built with native Illinois stone. The entry door is solid, and quite heavy. There's a grand *foyer* paneled with Norwegian pine, hand-carved moldings, and Waterford crystal chandeliers the size of a Volkswagen hung from the three-story high ceiling. And there's a winding staircase wide enough to drive a truck up leading to the second floor. It is, in a much overused word—*awesome.*

When Industrialist *John Olin* and his wife, *Adele Levis Olin*, moved into the home, the cost to construct it was about $600,000. This was in 1927. Today, to duplicate this home would cost somewhere between 30 and 35 MILLION; the land alone might be worth that much. I've not seen a home like this even on *"Lifestyles of the Rich and Famous."*

There are 14 bedrooms and 14 baths full baths. It sits on a knoll amid 32 acres of huge trees and magnificent landscaping overlooking the Mississippi River. You have a view of the river from every room.

Outside from the knoll, look left and you see the arches of St. Louis; look right and you see 15 miles down river; it is magnificent view and a totally unbelievable house.

John Olin lived to almost 90, and in the mid 1960's moved to St. Louis. He donated his River House to Southern Illinois University in 1975 and since, the home has had three owners; Coach has owned it TWICE.

The walls are TWO FEET THICK. There's a cedar closet the size of a very large den, the original doors have huge ball-bearing hinges that today cost about $400 EACH. I've never seen anything like it other *than Windsor Castle.*

Coach had the kitchen "modernized" but only with things like dishwasher, disposal, a refrigerator maybe ten or twelve feet long with several doors. The cabinetry was painted fresh but still with the "old" look from the twenties. Being IN the home was as if you were living in another era of time.

A DREAM COME TRUE

Coach and his wife Chriss, when he began to make *sizable* money with A.L. Williams, drove that curvy road past large mansions and looked at the front of the house, marveled at the size of it, at the pond, and at the landscaping.

They would drive several hundred feet below along the road bordering the Mississippi and look up.

He couldn't see much but trees, but he knew that "up there" was 32 wooded acres that surrounded that magnificent structure.

In the past, being nearly dirt-poor, it was only a dream, a fantasy, and for the most part far beyond the "reach" of a poor person. But when a dream becomes reality, you just have to be *proud* of yourself. I'M proud of him!

Coach's *entire* story can't be told in this book, but when you visit his office, there are scrap books, photo albums, posters, memorabilia and more.

URGE HIM to show you *The River House*; tell him I said to do it. He promised me that if anyone who read my book and visited his office, that he would show it to them.

I'm skipping parts of the story. Buying this magnificent mansion didn't just "happen." In fact that same "curvy road" that he took while looking at this huge house was similar to the same curvy road he took in life.

PART OF HIS LIFE

Coach married Rebecca in 1956. They had two sons, Scott and Frank; Frank is 2½ years younger than Scott. At the time of his marriage, Coach was just out of the service, 82nd Airborne and attending college in Anderson, Indiana. He was in the vending business for several years before he was "called to the ministry." This was 1966.

Coach took over as pastor of a small church, *The First Church of God,* in Benton, Illinois. Coach's first sermon was before 44 people; 14 were family and friends. His charisma and leadership skills impacted the church. Within a few years, (in a town of 6,000), he had 2,000 at the dedication of his new church. He and "*Beck*" loved working together as a team.

In 1972, six years after becoming pastor, Beck was diagnosed with cancer. For seven years she went through chemotherapy and Coach could only watch, be by her side, and pray for her. Sometimes the outcome looked good and other times bleak. Just days short of her 40th birthday, Rebecca left earth to reside with The Lord.

Coach, after guiding others for years, now needed guidance himself. "*Things just weren't the same without Beck. I haven't the heart to continue,*" Coach told the deacons, and he resigned as pastor.

You see, Rebecca and Coach were inseparable. When The Lord took her, Coach, heartbroken, felt that he could no longer serve the church as he once had and left the ministry with a $10,200 annual income.

RAGS TO RICHES

There are *so many* things to TELL about Coach; the love and the heartbreak that happens to most of us if we live long enough. But Coach actually "turned his life around" and then went forward to help others do the same thing.

It was 1980. Coach, now a widower, along with Scott who was 20 and Frank, not quite 18. With a combined income of a little over $30,000 a year, "stumbled" into a company that sold life insurance. His first two recruits were his sons.

They had no salary or GUARANTEE, they were paid on performance—on (as Scott puts it) *"what we were worth!"* The first two months the three Tomer's made NOTHING! The third month they made just over $1,000 and were excited. Over a period of time, Coach's final downline totaled more that 250,000 customers.

Here is an excerpt from a March 1983 article that appeared in *The Saturday Evening Post.* It was about our mentor, our friend, our "Coach."

"Lloyd Tomer, 48, from small-town Benton, Illinois, is one of the fastest-rising managers at A.L. Williams. Prior to licensing in April 1981, he was floundering. His wife died of cancer in 1979, he was an out-of-work minister with two children, and he had made just $10,200 in 1980. As a senior vice president with A.L. Williams, his 1982 income was more than $175,000."

Frank had a good head for business, and was a model student. Scott, on the other had, had less affinity for education and was kind of a "maverick."

On October 4, 1986 Coach married Chriss. They have a son, J. T. who is 18, and a seven-year-old daughter named Samantha. Coach had earned several million dollars with A.L Williams. In October of

1996, Coach BOUGHT *The River House*.

In 2001, Coach sold his downline in A.L. Williams (now called *Primerica*) to his son, Frank, and felt he would retire.

COACH DID SOME SOUL SEARCHING

Coach and Chriss enjoyed the magnificent mansion overlooking the Mississippi River. They now had the finances to enjoy the rest of a charmed life together.

Then one day, Coach (as many of us do) did some *soul-searching* and found that his life simply HAD to mean more than just getting rich and living well for the remainder of his life. He talked it over with Chriss and *"she stood by her man."*

Chriss loved that splendid home, but she loved her husband more. She knew that retirement wasn't for him, and that he had too much to offer the world other than to sit and watch time pass. She also knew that he had a *"need to be needed"* and, together, they made their decision.

It's a rather long story, but Coach, his son Scott and Coach's long-time friend Kim Sorensen got involved with Your Travel Biz. It costs a lot of money to start a new business, and especially featuring a network marketing company.

To MAKE the company work, Coach needed more investment capital and he SOLD his beloved River House in September of 2003. Coach put THAT money into YTB, the company I'm suggesting you at least "look into."

When Coach sold *The River House* it was with but one stipulation; that he get *first right of refusal* to buy it back—if the time ever came. Well, in November of 2006 Coach is moving BACK into *The River House*.

There is so very MUCH to be told about Coach that there truly isn't room in this book for it all. When you decide to get more "involved" in this company you'll learn much more of his background and accomplishments. You'll learn WHY this has"worked" for so many, and how it *could work* for you.

TOOLS

The company has a SUCCESS magazine (with a CD inside) that is marvelous. I've seen magazines and I've seen *magazines,* but *this one* is SPECTACULAR in every sense. It has COLOR photos of a hundred or so people with some terrific stories by *notables.*

Some of the information IN this magazine is in this book. I didn't mean to steal anything or plagiarize but I certainly "borrowed" some of my info from it because I get information wherever I can. To be legal, I call it "research."

Oh, did I ever tell you how Coach got his name *Coach?* J. Lloyd Tomer (Coach's given name; the J stands for James) had a colleague in his insurance business who was a team player and a superior businessman named J.(James) Kim Sorensen, one of the two other partners who started this business.

They were having a discussion, and when Lloyd was talking and Kim butted in. *"Do you want to COACH or BE coached?"* Lloyd asked his friend. Without hesitation, Kim said, *"BE coached, Coach!"* The name stuck.

Only his friends *prior to* YTB call him Lloyd. I call him Coach. I did call him Lloyd a few days ago on the telephone and it didn't "sound" right to me. I'll call him Coach. It fits him.

This isn't the last you'll hear about Coach. As we move along through this book I'll tell you more. Let's look at *Scott* Tomer and see what he is "made of."

THE APPLE FELL UNDER THE TREE

This is a case where *"the apple fell right **under** the tree,"* concerning Coach's eldest son, Scott. There's no doubt that Coach is the one who is most seen and heard in YTB, but Scott is right "up there" too.

Scott was Coach's first *recruit* in the A.L. Williams company. *"Scott was GIVEN nothing,"* Coach told me; *"he EARNED it! He is highly successful in his role as President and CEO of YTB. He proved to be a good teacher and organizer."*

Scott left A.L. Williams in 1992 to become a *Certified Financial Planner*, you know, the person who figures out what is best to do with your finances. He was grooming himself to do the job he now has. Scott and his dad have worked together in businesses several times, and when YTB was organized, Coach chose Scott to be CEO of YTB. Scott is a superb leader.

Scott is in his late forties but looks like he's in his early thirties. He stands straight (YOU judge here's his photo) whether he's "hard to look at" or not. I think he's better looking than Coach, and even Coach might admit that.

Yes, the "outside" of Scott is that of a tall, slim, happy person; good father, good husband, good Christian, and loving son who has *earned his right* to head this company.

Coach remarked several times to me, how proud he is of Scott and what a terrific job he is doing with YTB.

Scott came up to the podium dressed in very casual clothes (he dislikes suits and ties) and began to speak. Of course I didn't know WHAT to expect because (again) I've heard at least a THOUSAND speakers.

Scott "identified" with the crowd immediately. I don't recall his exact words, but he is COACH—only a few decades younger. I was looking at the crowd's reaction to what he was saying, and they actually LOVED him.

He was funny at times, sincere at other times, and moved almost to tears at still other times. He "reached" each and every person in that large room of about 300 people. He reached ME, and I too had tears well in my eyes over some of what he said.

In ALMOST the exact words in that SUCCESS magazine article, Scott tends to shy away from the spotlight, but he is a true worker. He's a "regular" guy that you can't help liking. He's one of the "ordinary people" who has accomplished extraordinary things.

Scott's mom died when he was 20. Gosh, when he tells how wonderful she was and how much he loved her, you have to know that his loss was great.

THE OTHER PERSON WHO HEADS YTB

There are three "main" characters in this story and J. Kim Sorensen is the third. I hadn't met him, but we've talked at length on the telephone and I LIKE the way he sounds. Coach praises him to the high heavens.

Kim is in charge of the TRAVEL in YTB, and travels the country giving speeches. He has a colorful background; he was a professional bowler until age 31, and then bought a bowling center.

Well, the bowling center went *belly up* in 1980 and so did Kim. In his own words; *"I drank everything I could find for six months, and then one day I found the Lord. I met Coach three months after—October*

1981. We've been close friends ever since."

Kim has had the same wife for 37 years and has three children and four grandchildren. Before YTB Kim owned his own businesses and managed a multi-million dollar government complex in Springfield, Illinois from 1973 to 1976.

He joined Coach in A.L. Williams in 1981 and designed and implemented many programs that helped that company succeed. He became a Senior VP with A.L. Williams. He moved from Springfield to St. Louis to join Coaches "team" in 1990.

J. Kim Sorenson

founder and president of YTB Travel Network of Illinois

Kim and Coach invested in a "travel business" with a company that was booking tours that tried networking. It didn't work out. So Kim flew to Florida to see what he could salvage of the money he and Coach had invested.

"I saw what that company had done wrong, and I felt that we could do it right. WE have with YTB. It started slow, but we feel we have made it and it will just get better". He added; "Coach and I have never had an argument. He, Scott and I have what we feel is a great team." (I agree wholeheartedly).

"This other company, Pete, tried doing business with an 800#. I knew that "word of mouth" (plus the Internet) was the way to make it work, I found Travelocity, the first online search engine in America booking air, hotel and cars. We have competitive prices and we do everything possible to assist our RTAs.

"I know you mention The River House and we used it to bring is as many as 40 people at a time; as a sort of showplace to get their attention. We would feed them, drive them wherever necessary. Yes. It IS quite a showplace," Kim finished.

And, I understood. It's just what you do, you know, show whatever you can to instill confidence in those you want to work for you. The River House is certainly a "confidence builder."

THE PERFECT BUSINESS

What IS the "perfect" business? Well, it's the business that YOU believe in. Of course you need the right *product,* but that's only the start. You also need several other "ingredients" to give yourself a *chance* to succeed.

I feel that because of my research, knowledge of businesses, having seen so many that failed and those that succeeded, that I KNOW what these necessary ingredients are.

ACADEMICALLY, the "perfect business" is one that is new or unique, has a product the masses want or need, that is used over and over again and that is EASY to market. It's also where the ones "running" the business have successful business experience, money, INTEGRITY, and where you are trained.

You already read the statistics as far as "travel" being a terrific business; the TREND points to more travel. You also know *some* of what you need to do to be successful in this business, so all that's left is for me to give you FACTS to convince you to join YTB.

FIRST, you have the PRODUCT that "the masses" want. A product that is a consumable, one that people use time and time again. This builds RESID-UAL income; income that pays you while you're asleep, on vacation, sick or you just want to take off. You can't do that with LINEAR income.

LINEAR income is what you get with a job. When YOU stop work, the MONEY stops. If you want to earn more money from your job, work faster or work longer hours.

SECOND, you need to know how much you are going to earn for marketing this product. And, are you willing to put in the time to LEARN about it and to actually DO it?

THIRD is the company itself. Do the corporate offices have integrity, business experience, money (to sustain a business if there are mistakes)? Do they truly CARE about those who work with and for them?

That CARE word is "thrown around" by MOST companies and most do NOT truly care; they care OK, but about their profit or their stockholders.

And finally, are you TRAINED to market this product? How much TIME does it take to learn about it, and can ANYBODY do it without a college degree or having to be a salesperson? How much support do you get from the company, and is it FUN to do or is it stressful SELLING?

Well, it's certainly FUN to make money, and MORE fun to spend it. You sincerely need all four of these things to make your business successful and then, you must have the DESIRE to make money, FOCUS on how to do it, and then PERSEVERE.

YTB It is TOTALLY unbelievable! The more I read the more EXCITED I became. I am excited as I write about it and I'm anxious to see those of you who read this book to join YTB.

GUARANTEE

Here's that "guarantee" word again. Can I guarantee that YOU will get rich in this business or even make an additional $500 per month? **NO and YES!** What I mean is that neither I nor anyone can guarantee you'll get rich. But THIS company does GUARANTEE that you'll earn at least $6,000 a year IF you follow what they prescribe.

Can YOU earn a MILLION DOLLARS? **MAYBE, but probably NOT**; the odds aren't in your favor. But there are several in YTB who are making a million dollars and more. So, it's POSSIBLE.

IT JUST MAKES SENSE

This is short book but there's a long story behind this company. The product is there, the pay-plan is good, the corporate officers are the best I have EVER found, and the training is there.

If you have a computer and know even a little about the Internet, you can start your OWN home-based business with YTB in minutes. You need NO prior education or training, you need little (or NO) money to try, and you're in business for yourself.

As I read over what I've written, I seem to be *"pushing you"* on these YTB businesses—and I AM. I am not being paid to do this book and if you join or not will make little difference to me financially.

It's a fact, that these guys are "real" people. No pretense. No flash. They (usually) dress the way I do on my ranch Also, they have "been there." Those running this company can, *"Talk the talk,"* because *"they have walked the walk."*

This is not an "ordinary" company; the ones "running it" have been successful working in this type of business. They KNOW what to do and what NOT to do. They have watched many of their friends lose money and lose faith, and it broke their hearts seeing this. They are doing it CORRECTLY!

Travel AGENCIES are closing daily. People are traveling more often, and if you can get them competitive fares, you're in business.

*"If you don't TAKE a chance,
you never HAVE a chance!"*

THERE IS NO CHANCE

YTB put in a "Bill of Rights" in the associates contract that **GUARANTEES** you'll be paid what you earn and that they will NOT change their marketing plan. It's written and registered.

Just about EVERY network marketing company

(on the back of their contract in very small print) has the *Terms & Conditions* which STATE that "the company has the RIGHT to change the marketing plan." Those of you who are not "new" to this business know that's true. If not, LOOK at a contract and see.

I have reported my findings to you. I feel it is a great CHANCE for YOU—no matter what your financial situation is or how many times you've failed before—to change your life for the better, forever.

My research was so very rewarding to me. I'm writing this book because I like to help people succeed. I will, personally, help YOU with this business. If you follow what you're taught, the ONLY reason you won't succeed is if you stop trying or quit.

I know that ANYONE CAN DO IT if they have the desire, focus and the right "vehicle." THIS is that vehicle. You can feel safe and secure with ALL of it.

Whether you become involved or not is your choice. When you do finish this book, please give it to someone you care for.

The only reason YTB won't DOUBLE their business in the months ahead, double it again and double THAT again, is if their REPs and RTAs stop TELLING about it.

PROGRESS

They began YTB on two floors of a downtown Alton, Illinois bank (shown above) their first 2½ years and then 1½ years in the building shown below.

HERE is where their NEW offices will be: a K-MART building and parking area!

And THIS is the drawing of their NEW offices. They have MOVED INTO 20,000 square feet of it in December, 2006. AND, there's an additional 100,000 square feet of space they are "working on."

Look at the PROGRESS and what these individuals "running" this company have made. Their growth cycle started off in a "reasonable" fashion. Then they got better and BETTER and **BETTER.**

SHOOT FOR THE STARS is a good name for

this book. YTB "shot for the stars" and is reaching higher. Now it's YOUR chance to do the same. Yes, now it's YOUR turn to SHOOT FOR THE STARS!

Not only that, but statistics point out that MORE people have become millionaires in Network Marketing in the past twenty years than all other businesses combined.

Please don't let this word "millionaire" persuade or discourage you; your chances of becoming a millionaire are rare—but possible. I just want you to TRY these businesses on a part-time basis. When you are earning a few thousand per month, then decide whether to keep your JOB or not.

Again, statistics say that NINETY-SIX percent of adults between the ages of 25 and 45 have "looked" into starting their own business. But REMEMBER, you must have the PRODUCT that "the masses" use, and use over and over again to produce RESIDUAL income. Then look at the pay plan, corporate officers who know what they're doing and whom you can TRUST, and then the training. YTB HAS IT ALL!

I truly have neither seen nor even *heard of* a company that has all of it; an outstanding product that just about everyone uses, an *extremely* lucrative pay plan, competent and proven leadership and so much truly good training.

And, it you're willing to really TRY, I'll help you. E-mail me for my FREE Information Packet. If you're serious about this business and willing to TRY, I'm available anytime.

Chapter 6

ALL ABOUT MONEY

This is my FAVORITE CHAPTER! It's the reason so many are pursuing their own home-based business; for the money, for *extra* money, or for a CHANCE to guarantee their financial security.

Again, I can't GUARANTEE you any money; I don't know you, how much time you'll put in, how smart you are, how strong your desire is to make money or any of these things.

What I can promise is that YOU are the only guarantee. I'll help you, these Directors will help you, Coach will help, the "tools" I spoke about earlier will help you. In fact, there is so much HELP that I am astounded. You see, if WE help you, and YOU help others; EVERYBODY WINS!

HERE are but *some* of the wonderful "perks" about YTB. THIS is what you can expect if you become a REP with this company.

☆**A $6,000 GUARANTEE:** THIS has never been done before (to my knowledge) in the history of network marketing companies. A GUARANTEE of a minimum of $6,000 in as few as twelve months. This isn't much money, I realize that, but it is a GUARANTEE.

Years ago, when I decided to write about working a business from your home, my "aim" was to help people make an *additional* $500 a month. THIS amount of money would make a major difference in the lives of 95% of the people in the world.

I also mentioned that about 85% of the people who are IN network marketing make expenses, earn no money, or they *lose* money. That, of course, is because most don't understand the business but more so because they never "work" the business.

I think the "average" number of people contacted BY those in a home-based business is less than THREE! How in the world can anyone make money selling anything if they contact but three people? It's possible, but highly unlikely.

With YTB, if you give out 25 of their SUCCESS magazines a month and "follow up" with but one single telephone call, for twelve months and you haven't earned $6,000, **YTB will write you a check for the DIFFERENCE!** They aren't lying to you; they will do it.

The "trick is" they are playing the odds. Their reasoning is if anyone gives out 25 of those magazines per month and follows up with a telephone call the "law of averages" comes into play and they simply CANNOT make but $6,000 for the year.

It truly isn't trickery, it's a fact. If they can prompt you to reach for that "$6,000 carrot" they are (in a fashion) FORCING you to work. And you "should" make many times more than $6,000.

WORK WORKS! SMART work works better. And HARD, SMART work has the best chance of paying off. And LUCK hardly comes into play. The person who "has so much" wasn't lucky; they WORK-ED for it. And the person who worked the hardest usually has the most!

What I ask you to do is make a "game" of it and it IS no longer work. NOW, let's talk about MORE of the BENEFITS in YTB.

☆**$1,000 and $10,000 BONUSES:** This is an easy one. But please follow this closely. Once YOU are a REP you are (personally) required to enroll three RTAs. You must then (either you or any of the three) enroll a total of six. THIS sets up your "power team." The next persons that YOU personally enroll, start you off on a bonus.

Every time six RTAs are sold in your REP Power Team—every time—you earn a $1,000 bonus. Yes, six RTAs in your first team, you start your power team.

I realize it seems like a LOT of people, but it's really NOT; that "exponential growth" business takes over. Everyone they get in, everyone *they* get in and on and on, and you total 100 RTAs, you get an **additional** bonus of $10,000 **every time** your "power team" gets in another 100 RTAs.

Again, there's much to tell and much to learn about WHY I feel YTB is for ANYONE. When you talk to the person who gave you this book, ask THEM to explain it, one-on-one, instead of my confusing you.

When you have 500 RTAs in your REP Power Team, you become a Director and your benefits include:

☆**$100,000 LIFE INSURANCE POLICY:** When your total team reaches 500 RTAs, the company **GIVES YOU** a life insurance policy worth $100,000.

☆**FREE MEDICAL INSURANCE:** When you work with all MLM companies, you are an "independent contractor." This means that if you want medical insurance, you have to BUY it. With YTB, when you get 500 RTAs you are GIVEN **FREE MEDICAL INSURANCE.**

☆**$24,000 A YEAR, MINIMUM EXTRA INCOME GUARANTEED:** In addition to commissions and bonuses, you will get a minimum of $2,000 a month as a DIRECTOR. You become a director when you get that 500 RTA "magic number," and give ONE MEETING a month. That's an additional $24,000 a year for conducting but 12 meetings.

☆**$1,000,000.00 BONUS:** Think that's a typo? WHO in this world gets a **ONE MILLION DOLLAR BONUS? Unheard of, huh?**

Remember the guy I mentioned briefly at the beginning of this book, Ron Head? He and his wife Judy, In YTB about 4½ years, were awarded their million dollar BONUS at the Red Carpet Days meeting. I was THERE! I SAW the check.

☆**$50,000 BONUS:** There were 12 REPs who EACH received a BONUS for $50,000. I haven't room for their photos, but you'll meet them ALL when you join this team.

The LEADERS

Ron & Judy Head

Camaron & Jamie Corr

"PJ" Jensen

Rick & Brenda Ricketts

Bill & Anne Hoffmann

Juliet St. John

Jerome Hughes & Katrina Greenhill

Dave & Marlis Funk

Floyd & Carla Williams

James & Marcia Prewitt

Steve Branch & TV Wilson

Arlyne Thompson

Kent & Kim McLaughlin

Not EVERYONE will get a MILLION DOLLAR BONUS; just the few who work hard and smart and have FUN doing their business.

But these GUARANTEES on each six and each hundred RTAs in your "Power Team" is highly possible which is NOT an unattainable goal. I MET many of these folks at . . .

RED CARPET DAYS

This happens almost EVERY Thursday at the YTB office just outside St. Louis when two to three hundred people show up from all over the U.S. (including Hawaii and Alaska). Coach treats them to a luncheon at the country club and there is somewhat of a meeting that is more like a friendly get-together.

This is the time that the *REPs and RTAs* bring along their family and friends to SHOW OFF their business. When I attended there were about 300 people. NOW, five months later, there were 1,300.

The day that I visited was somewhat special; TODAY was a milestone in YTB. You see, it took about FIVE YEARS to build up to 20,000 RTAs. Mathematically, with the way new RTAs had come into the business, their "magic number" was 52,269 by the year 2007.

An hour BEFORE the luncheon, the company HIT their goal two and a half months BEFORE the deadline. And Coach had money set aside for an early CHRISTMAS BONUS for his 129 employees.

Coach TRIPLED their bonus, and the REPs who were "big money-earners" got together and added enough money out of THEIR OWN POCKETS to *quadruple* their bonuses!

Their idea was to thank the employees of YTB for all their support. These employees helped THEM make what I feel are astronomical checks. And they wanted to SHARE their success with those who helped them! It IS one large, loving, caring family, the likes of which I had NEVER seen in over FORTY YEARS of being "around" these companies.

EACH employee got a check; even ones who had worked there but a few months or a few WEEKS. Of course, the longer you were there the bigger the bonus. But these employees, one by one, came up as their name was called and received their checks. Some were so happy and so thankful that they cried; it was a warm and wonderful thing to experience.

These Christmas bonus checks ranged from six hundred dollars to several THOUSAND. Sandy (Pippins) and several other long-term employees received **$6,000 bonus checks**.

"*You might not make big money,*" Coach and Kim told Sandy when they were starting YTB, "*but we're going to have a lot of fun.*" Sandy accepted the job. Now, she is an integral part in the success of the company

She knew Coach and Kim. She knew they had integrity, and would make YTB successful. And I feel she also knew that if THEY made it, SHE would be compensated.

I met Kim at Coach's Birthday Bash. I'd already heard only GOOD things about him from everyone who knew him. He and Coach are alike. Each are good men who love the Lord, their family, people and they love life. I think in that order.

The speakers at this luncheon were ALL interesting. First was *Andrew F. Cauthen* (Andy) who is their Chief Operations Officer. He was a terrific speaker with a personality that everyone seems to like.

Then came Scott to the podium. There were other speakers; corporate officers, key personnel and some of the associates who received big checks.

As for meetings, conventions, company "get-togethers," they are almost all the same. **NOT THIS TIME!** Please understand, I have sat in hundreds of luncheons, conventions and meetings. Some are so repetitious and downright boring that If I had a gun, I'd SHOOT myself! THIS ONE held my attention throughout; ALL the speakers were truly good.

I often say to presidents of these various companies that if they have a big-money-earner who can speak, let them speak. The ones who can't—give them their award, pat them on the back, let them wave at the audience and get them **OUT OF THE WAY!**

When the day ended, I had met dozens of the associates and applauded the speakers and leaders. MOST OF ALL I got to "know" more about WHY this business is so special. It starts at the top and moves down. It was like one large FAMILY! YTB is special. It truly **IS** ONE BIG FAMILY!

A MILLION DOLLAR BONUS

I was THERE! I saw the CHECK! Ron and Judy Head were given a MILLION DOLLARS! WHO does THAT? I've not seen nor heard of ANY company giving one of their REPs a million dollar BONUS check. If they got that much as a "bonus" I was a bit hesitant to ask Ron or Judy what their MONTHLY check was.

I saw Rick Ricketts. I had met him ten or so years before when he was with another company. Rick and Brenda are the largest money-earners in YTB. Their income for this year (2006) is right at TWO (plus) MILLION dollars. He and another RTA named P.J. Jensen are due to get their ONE MILLION DOLLAR BONUS just before Christmas, 2006.

I talked to Rick a few minutes ago over the telephone from his gorgeous home in Florida. I called the day before but he was "on the road" flying some-place to give **one** of his team members a $50,000 bonus check!

"Pete," Rick said, "*you and I have been around this business for many years. I've never known such a company existed as this one. As you say, the product is outstanding and easy to sell but the leadership is phenomenal!*

"*Coach, Scott, Kim, Andy, Sandy; they are all truly talented, caring individuals. THEY are the reason this company is successful. But, as you know, there is* work involved. I put in as much effort today as I did when I started in September of 2002. It's become second nature to me."

Rick KNOWS this business. *"You can sell product,"* Rick said, *"and you'll make money doing it, but the BIG money is when you find several good people, train them to duplicate **your** efforts and the matching bonuses and residual income is there.*

"It's easy to talk to others about a home-based business when the product makes sense. You know the 80/20 rule; 20% of the people do 80% of this business. I just call them, try to motivate and reason with them, and it works."

"Kiss enough frogs, and you'll find a Prince"

MILLIONAIRES IN YTB

P.J. (Pete) Jensen, former quarter back for Iona College in New York, also played football in the NFL with the New York Jets and the Giants, as well as two years in Europe. "My success with YTB grows with the success of others."

I met him at the Birthday Bash. He has a tremendous personality, is a really terrific leader and is better looking than his picture.

P.J. (Pete)Jensen, millionaire!

Rick and Brenda Ricketts, millionaires!

Ron and Judy Head, millionaires!

*Juliet St. John,
millionaire!*

When Coach met Juliette she was sleeping in her car. Within one year with YTB she retired her mother. She received the Ruby President's Club ring ($500,000 in earnings in a 12-month period and is now a MILLIONAIRE!

MORE MONEY TALK

This entire chapter is about MONEY. I've "*danced around*" telling you about this travel business, why you should be involved with it, my own "sad stories" about not having any *money* (then having it, losing it and making it again) and I mention MONEY an awful lot.

I tell about Coach having so little MONEY, then how much MONEY he made with A.L. Williams, how much MONEY it took to start this business, how much MONEY his River House cost to build back in 1927, and how much MONEY it would take to build it today.

Also, how much MONEY some of these leaders have made. Yeah, like it or not, this book is about

MONEY! The title of this book (SHOOT FOR THE STARS), isn't about being an astronomer or an astronaut or about NASA, it's about MONEY.

I tell about how much *money* is spent on travel, how much (money) it cost to advertise, how much (money) it takes to start a business, how much (MONEY) some others have made, etc., etc.

ALSO, as I look over this entire book, I have not misrepresented, hedged, fudged, exaggerated or LIED to you one single time—about ANYTHING.

Coach told me two things when we met; two "standards" he lives by, preaches and demands of those around him (if they want to remain his friend or continue working in this business):

> *"If it ain't true, don't say it,"*
> and
> *"If it ain't right, don't DO it."*

I've followed these two tenets in this entire book. BUT let's get down to the "meat and potatoes" of this book; it's about MONEY. More specifically how much MONEY you can make in this business.

Since I vow to *"tell it like it is"* we are ALL interested in how much MONEY we can make. IMPORTANT? I'd say so. I think in order to have a "good" life your health is certainly important, but, MONEY is close behind. Needing money is no fun, but being rich *then becoming* poor is DEVASTATING! I've *been there*, remember?

Continuing on about money (I must mention MONEY *at least* a hundred times in this book), money is important. But MONEY is not the *"root of all evil,"* it's the LOVE of money that is. If YOU make big money in this business—please help others. And, by HELPING others you help yourself!

A friend of mine after his divorce, was despondent because his wife of twenty years, and his four kids, were not *around* anymore. He was also left with very little money—several reasons to be unhappy.

BUT, he inherited some *money* and his attitude changed for the better. He seemed to be happier now with money. Trying to make the best of it he told me something that I'll never forget . . .

> *"Money doesn't buy happiness,*
> *but it makes MISERY easy to endure."*

HUMAN NATURE

Most people want to know; *"How can you help ME (lose weight, get rid of wrinkles, live longer, be healthy, find a mate, buy a car at the best price, **make money,** etc.) I've tried several home-based business and have had rotten luck with all of them. WHY is this business different?"* This isn't a selfish question; it's human nature and a good question.

It's a fact that MOST divorces are over *money.* Most MURDERS are over *money.* Almost all robberies and burglaries are over money. And many partnerships end because of money. I've been rich and I've been poor and I prefer rich.

Yes, money has caused many problems. Friendships and partnerships often end over MONEY. When partnerships do badly, they blame each other because they didn't make any money. Conversely, when they MAKE money (many times) either one or the other wants to take CREDIT and the partnership (and the friendship) dissolves.

THAT'S what's so great about this business. You can MAKE money, you can SAVE money, and you can help OTHERS make and save money. And hopefully, they in turn, will do as you have done and help others. Then EVERYBODY MAKES MONEY.

MAKE MONEY WITH A SYSTEM

Many people that I knew who became successful in network marketing began with very little or NO money, but found a product and a company they believed in. They learned about the product, developed a "system" that suited *their* personality, and they worked it hard and smart.

I want you to USE a system that *you* like. OF COURSE listen to the leaders, but if you can't do EVERYTHING they suggest, pick out what suits YOUR personality, practice doing it over and over again, then start telling others about it.

Your leaders are SPECIAL people. They worked their own "system" and it worked for them. If it works for you, DUPLICATE it and teach others how to do it.

I was the keynote speaker at a huge convention of about 15,000 in Norway several years ago. A business I had written a book about had helped the 24 people who were on stage make MILLIONS.

I was trying to get a point across to the audience, and if you know my rotten personality, I poke fun at almost everyone (and also at myself). I told the audience, "If you don't think YOU can't make it in this business, just LOOK at this sorry bunch up here who are ALL millionaires. If THEY can make it, ANYONE can!"

With YTB, there IS no certain height, weight, age, color of hair, skin, religion—NOTHING to identify these folks as leaders—they are certainly a diverse group and each makes a substantial amount of money.

The REASONS they hold these high positions are several; they *liked* the product, they *saw the opportunities*, they *learned* what to do, and they DID IT! It truly is THAT simple. That's why I say again and again ANYBODY CAN DO IT!

My reason for telling so much about MONEY is because the main reason people work in this business is because they know if they find a system they like and can perfect, the MONEY follows. Make it a GAME and have fun "winning" the game.

"To be successful,
you have to LIKE what you're doing,
and KNOW what you're talking about."

Here are names of MORE successful YTB associates; all Level one Directors. There are MORE since I began research on this book. When you "bump into them" at Red Carpet Days or at the convention, ask them about their business.

Kevin Adams, Preston and Jane Blair, Melissa Boston, Diane and Gary Adams, Malcolm Alexander, Michelle and Roland Athouris, Deborah and Donald Bradley, Barbara Braveboy-Locklear, Ron and Phyllis Bush, Searafin Cailles, Bob Campbell, Bill and Charlton, Georgia and Tim Dominey, Brenda and Lauren Dowlar, Irma and Bill Frye, Terry Graham, Tessie Graham, Bass Grant, Bwenny and Sharon Hampton, Keith Hipp, Spencer Iverson, Antijuan Jack, Ann Jones, Chuck King, Nick Nicholson, Von Niclleberry, Ann, Ottaviano, Cathy and Kirk Phinney, Elisa Pineiro and Samuel Gomez. Mickey and Dave Rawls, Joe Reid, Delvy Santiago, James "Bonecrusher" Smith, Denson Taylor, Charles and Franceina Thompson, Nancy and Victor Toyens

I was at a convention a few years ago when the president of that particular company gave a PHOTO of their new building for all who would sign up ($400) for the next year's convention.

At Coach's Birthday Bash, HE gave about 45 associates of YTB BONUSES totaling TWENTY-FIVE MILLION DOLLARS! It truly IS unbelievable at how fantastic this company is.

AUTHOR'S CLOSING COMMENTS

Well, if I haven't "beaten you down" with this YTB business, I certainly TRIED! I've written this book to give you FACTS, to try and appeal to your common sense judgment, and help you make an INFORMED decision.

There IS no promise or guarantee; YOU are the only guarantee and you must work hard, and SMART, but have FUN while doing it. I'll tell you HOW. I KNOW this business. Can YOU make a lot of money? Of COURSE you can. This is a great CHANCE to do it. And remember, I"LL HELP YOU!

The WEALTHY are rarely the ones who *come up* with an idea; it's the ones who *implement that idea who put it in MOTION!* Then comes, desire, focus, perseverance and a PRODUCT to market that makes sense in a company you can count on..

A. J. Foyt (famous race car driver), a friend who lives in Houston said: *"Luck is when opportunity meets preparation."* I'm not certain if he coined that phrase or copied it but it certainly is fact.

I used to say, *"Opportunity knocks but once, whereas temptation bangs away for years."* Cute saying but not necessarily true; OPPORTUNITY is everywhere, you just need to recognize it and DO it.

I always say (in several of my "business" books), **SW, SW, SW, N!** Some **WILL**, some **WON'T**, so **WHAT, NEXT!** This is a "people" business and a "numbers" game. TELL (never SELL) enough people and you will make extra money. How MANY you tell as well as how you *tell it* determines how much you earn.

Travel is a TERRIFIC *product* to TELL about.

There is almost THIRTY BILLION DOLLARS (a billion is a thousand MILLION) of money generated by retired persons, college students and stay-at-home moms working *from* home.

For more than TWENTY years I have been writing and preaching (teaching, I think) people to start their own home-based business.

I've taken enough of your time "setting up" what I feel is of utmost important to you; MUCH of what I've written many of you already know, I'm just re-reminding you of a few things.

In this business, in YTB, it is a "total" package. Coach, Scott, Kim, Sandy, Andy, ALL the corporate folks, as well as the leaders on down to those who just joined, all seem like true *family* to me.

When 129 employees get a TRIPLE Christmas bonus for the outstanding work they've done, and when the ASSOCIATES give them an additional bonus for helping them—that's FAMILY. I've NEVER seen anything like it in my life.

How very pleased I am to have "found" these people, this business, and this product that gives EVERYONE a chance to change their financial life forever. I've done "my job," now is the time for YOU to "step up to the plate" and do yours!

Good luck and God bless,
Pete Billac

ABOUT THE AUTHOR

PETE BILLAC is one of the most sought-after speakers in the United States. He has written 58 books; 46 have become best-sellers. His worldwide best seller, HOW NOT TO BE LONELY, sold more than SEVEN million copies. His books are published worldwide in 14 languages.

Pete is a maverick; he writes what pleases him. His topics range from adventure to war, the Mafia, famous people, romance, love, health, motivation, and business.

He speaks to Fortune 500 companies on marketing, he lectures at universities across America, and delivers his "message" at conventions and seminars around the world. For fun, he conducts lectures on cruise ships. Pete really ENJOYS helping others. He travels the world lecturing.

Perhaps you've seen Pete on Donahue, Sally Jessy Raphael, Good Morning America, Laff Stop or other national televison shows. He mixes common sense and knowledge with laughter. He charms his audiences with his winning smile, quick wit and candor, and breathes life into every topic. He makes his audiences laugh—hard!

"Pete is an expert at restoring self-confidence and self-esteem in others . . ."

Phil Donahue
National Television Talk Show Host

"The ladies were so taken with Mr. Billac's seminar, they were screaming for him to be the featured speaker at our Thirty-Fifth Annual Awards Dinner . . ."

Ouida DeBruhl
Mid-States Women's Conference

SHOOT for the STARS

TRAVEL, HAVE FUN, MAKE MONEY AND HELP OTHERS

Swan Publishing
Southwind Ranch
1059 CR 100
Burnet, TX 78611

(512) 756-6800
Fax (512) 756-0102

Visit our web site at: swan-pub.com
E-mail: pete@swan-pub.com

FOR MORE INFORMATION:

After reading this book, please pass it on to a friend or relative. It could change their financial lives forever!